101+ Ways To Quickly Make $1000

A Proven collection of income generating ideas for those who need fast cash

Check out some other recent titles from us

**How to Write
30 Books In 30 Days**

**Power Profits
Cash Flow Revolution**

**The 10 Principals of
ENDLESS WEALTH**

**The 10 Principals of
IT WORKS**

About the author

Danial Barron Howe is the author of over 350 books (under multiple pen names) ranging from business and online income to health and wellness. He is the founder of six multinational businesses including **2ndEmpireMedia**, the publisher of this book and TheMinuteMarketer.Com, a rapidly growing community catering to the ongoing education of information marketers.

Dan has been involved in the information marketing business ever since he wrote his first book, *POWER PROFITS!* Nearly a decade and a half ago. Since that time he has gone on to sell over 750,000 books in both printed and electronic form as well as numerous audio, video and other hybrid forms of informational products.

In addition to his role as an informational product producer, he holds several degrees including a Masters in mechanical engineering and design as well as degrees in psychology and biomechanics. He is a lifelong tinkerer artist and visionary innovator with a passion for improving efficiencies of systems such as those found within this book.

Forward

Can you really make 1000 quickly?
Believe it or not, the answer is *"yes"*! Most of the time people are so caught up in the problem of needing money that they let it blind them to the opportunities that surround them every day. .

Why should you listen to me?
I am a chronic workaholic, multi track serial entrepreneur who never seems to sit still for very long or stay focused on any one thing for any extended period of time. And on top of it all, I'm dyslexic too! Despite this, I still managed to author over 350 books in under 24 months without the use of subcontractors or virtual assistants! If I can achieve this level of output despite my hectic schedule, I'm quite confident you can do the same – *or even better!*

I can't write your books for you, nor can I market them for you. What I *will do* is teach you how to develop a group of ideas and get them all into book form incredibly quickly. My techniques above all else are what will separate you from those that never seem to get anything finished or put out for public consumption, despite otherwise having very marketable ideas.

What you can expect from this book.
I created this book as a personal challenge to myself. I wanted to sit down and pour out every idea I had for making money into one comprehensive collection for my dedicated readers. I've grown tired of hearing people say *"it's hard to make money"* or "I can't find a way to pay my bills each month". Beliefs like those are nothing more than self-made prisons. This book will present you the key

I promise you this: The methods I will give you here in this book will unlock a wellspring of ideas and a geyser of creativity! By the time you finish this book *you will have a series of workable ideas for creating no less than $1000, $2000, $5000 a month (or even way more)* if you choose to.

I am a full-time information marketer and author. Let me be clear upfront; I am not going to fill your head full of theoretical nonsense or recycled gibberish that I've pulled from various places all over the Internet. *I am a full time professional information marketer and 350+ title book author.* I'm in the trenches each day earning a living by the skills that I've acquired over a decade and a half of actual use. I know a thing or two about how to find money when I need it most. I have to, this is how I feed myself and my family! If you are looking for straightforward, candid advice on what works then follow me, I will get you where you want to go!

Index

Preface

What does it takes to make money these days?
The world may have changed but the principles of
wealth creation have not. These days things are come at
us faster and faster than ever before. We expect instant
results in every facet of our lives. In many of us this
breeds an expectancy that in turn creates a paradox (and
a financial problem) for them... one wonders *"How can
I make quick money?"* and ironically these people
spend years of unproductive time trying to answer that
question in an attempt to find a shortcut!

This book is filled with real host to goodness, tried and
true workable ideas. There is however one catch – they
all require work. You won't find shortcuts, cheats and
or promises of instant results here. That's how things
work – even in our instant gratification society

The good news is that by using any one (or a
combination of many) of the ideas found inside you'll
set yourself up for success and easily exceed the
promise the title of this book makes. The key is to never
give up.

British Prime Minister Winston Churchill, famously
addressed a graduating class. When asked to speak he
stood up, walked to the podium, quietly surveyed the
crowd in attendance and instead of delivering an
expectedly long winded speech, he simply announced
*"Never give up! Never give up! **Never, _ever_ give up!**"*
and with that he returned to his seat.... nuff said.

Building an action plan.
It may seem obvious to many of you, but understanding that never giving up is the key to success is what will change everything. You may have to cycle through *literally hundreds* of ideas before you find one you are well suited to that will carry you for many years.

The misunderstanding many people have is to expect to discover *a single one size fits all idea* that will produce a flood of income year after year. Yes, it can happen but it's not very often. So that generally speaking, that type of thinking won't get you very far.

To be a successful you must have *many hooks (income generating events) in the water* as possible at any given time. When it comes to making money, *volume rules!*

My advice here is simple; start with what interests you most. Some ideas will make you a little bit of money, some may make you none - while still others could make you a small fortune!

As for me, I can say without a doubt that developing informational products and eBooks and then marketing them through my various sales channels such as my websites, blogs, Youtube videos and yes, even fiverr as well has been an ongoing challenge and a thrill for me. It fits my personality and my lifestyle.

Sure, there was a learning curve with all of it, there always is. But, once I crossed that threshold into knowledge and proficiency I was able to enjoy a lifestyle that few will ever able to experience. When you find that thing that suits you well don't be afraid to dig deep and learn all there is to know. That depth of knowledge will help you rise to the top of

If you desire a life filled with more free time, the ability to apply your creativity in myriads of ways and a potentially far better rate of pay then you're currently earning, remember the words of Winston Churchill; *"Never give up! Never give up! Never, ever give up!"*

Ready? Then let's get started!

Chapter 1
Cashing in with your home

There's so many ways to use your house to make money, it's just mind blowing. I'm going to be very specific here by what I mean when I say *"using your house"* to make money. I don't mean finding spare change under the sofa cushion or anything like that. I mean using your house *as the asset that it truly is* instead of *the liability it will become* if you don't pay your rent/mortgage.

This isn't intended to be a crash course on economics, but I'll explain it to you the way a very wise man explained it to me…

When you stop "working" (aka earning a paycheck), **assets feed you** and **liabilities eat you**.

Let's look at your house for our case study.

If you (or whoever pays the bills at your residence) suddenly stopped paying the rent/mortgage, you would quickly realize that by the definition above, your house is a liability

Let's have a look at the flip side…

If you lost your job or stopped earning a paycheck but had people paying you rent to stay at your house, you'd be able to continue to pay the rent/mortgage. And if you kept your expenses intact, you'd even have profits left over. That's when your house would be an asset.

And that's the very first way of the 101+ ways to make $1,000, we'll discuss first.

Renting a room – you can easily make $250 per week by renting out rooms at your home. If you live in a highly desirable area, you can charge even more and probably make $250 a night. In 4 weeks or 4 days, you'll have that $1,000.

Now of course, you want to make sure that this is legal and all that stuff. I'm not an attorney. I'm just giving you friendly advice that has worked for thousands of others and me.

Here's a few services that streamline this process for you:

Airbnb

Kidandcoe (Same as Airbnb but exclusively for families and you can make more money)

Here's another way you can use your house to make money:

Renting out space – people ALWAYS need storage. You can charge people to store stuff at your house. A spare bedroom or basement would work perfectly.

You probably have a friend or family member that needs your help with this right now. A few boxes in an area of the house you're not using anyway are a perfect idea when you need some fast cash. Also, think about those self-storage places. They make an absolute fortune. You would be solving a huge problem for people. Cha-ching!

Try posting an ad for this on Craigslist and start interviewing or try this:

Sparechair (Launching soon. The twist here is people can use your space to work at home without being at their homes. The company is looking to help people network by making co working fun and profitable. You can charge $10-$20 a day)

Peerspace (If your space is creatively designed and can allow for groups of people to work then consider this)

You can even rent out areas of your home to filmmakers and producers:

Setscouter

3. Renting out your garage – somebody needs to store their car in your garage. If your garage is relatively clean (or can be made so), this is a really easy way to make some extra cash.

Not to get too shady here, but people sometimes need to hide their cars more than they need to store them. It can be a divorce, a debt collector, or even an angry former friend that forces someone's car into hiding. It can even be someone who wants to avoid parking on the street and subjecting themselves to parking permits. Help these people out and let them store their car in your garage.

Carmanation (Only available in San Francisco, California but expanding nationally soon)

You can use your house to make money this way too:

4. Renting out your driveway – if you live nearby a theater, stadium, park or any other large public meeting space, you can make plenty of money by renting out your driveway.

All you have to do is keep abreast of events in your area and set up an online advertisement of some sort and you'll get plenty of inquiries. You'll probably run out of parking spaces before you run out of people looking for them.

Here's another tip for this one: put up some corrugated signs before the event and write the words "Overflow Parking."

Depending on the event, you may be able to get someone to rent for a weekend or even a few more days. Remember you're solving a problem.

People *WILL PAY* for convenience!

Here's a source to check out for renting out your driveway and garage:

Justpark

5. Rent your car, bike, boat, outdoor equipment & extra land – If you're not using it then why not make money off it as an asset? You could be making $250 a week from that nice bike you bought last

Christmas or rent your extra car out and make an extra $2,000 a month.

For your bike, snowboard & surfboard:

Spinlister

For your car:

Relayrides

Getaround

For your boat:

Boatbound

For your outdoor equipment:

Outdoors

For your extra land for campers:

Gamping

6. Get paid to save energy – This company is looks to pay you to reduce your electricity at certain times and it's completely free. In a nutshell, all you need to do is turn off a couple things when they send you texts. Then you'll receive points which add up. After that all you need to do is click their "cash out" button on their dashboard. It's simple as that. You won't make a lot but $5 to $20 here and there can add up.

To learn more visit:

Ohmconnect

Chapter 2
Put Your Skills To Work

Okay… it's time for a pep talk. Some of you need this and some of you think you don't. If you're reading this, it wouldn't hurt to read it anyway.

Here's the deal… you might not think you have any skills. It would probably be more accurate to say that you might not think that you have any skills that other people will PAY for.

I can assure you of one thing…

If you believe that you don't have any skills that other people will pay for, you're DEAD WRONG. Simple and plain. That mindset is what's keeping you from making the money you really want to make.

Don't buy it?

Ok, let me play Devil's Advocate for a minute and agree with you. Let's say you really don't have any skills that anyone else will pay you for. Even if that's true (which it isn't), who says you can't acquire a particular skill and find people who need you to solve that problem for them?

See? You HAVE NO EXCUSE for being broke.

Remember… you don't have to be Ph.D. level proficient at a particular skill to make money with that skill. You literally only need to be a step or two ahead of the people you're helping and you'll be seen as an authority to them.

Realistically speaking, people want to be helped by people who are closer to their level. Having said that, let's get into some of the ways you can put your skills to work.

7. Consultation – if you've ever had some success or failures (because you can save them time and money) in:

Business

Technology

Sales/marketing

Skills/management

Funding projects

Products and design

Then there's a high chance someone will pay to learn what you know. You can make $1-$10 a minute which is roughly $60-$600 an hour using some of these services:

Clarity

Liveperson (Similar to clarity but with other niches)

Justanswer (Having credentials and degrees helps for this one)

Ether

This next resource is a bit similar but encompasses a few different niches such as:

Art & music

Computer & electronics

Cooking

Education & careers

Fashion & beauty

Fitness & nutrition

Health

Home & garden

People providing services on here are making $15-$200 an hour:

Helpouts.google.com

This one has everything and you can set your own amounts per project. If you're good why wouldn't you charge $200-$400 a gig? Don't think you're good? Then start slowly and raise your rates every so often.

Thumbtack

Tinkertask

8. Drive People Around – The days of investing money to purchase a taxi business have changed. Today you can freely partner up with a driving company and make $200-500 a day driving people with your own car. If you're worried about insurance these companies take care of it all. The cool thing about this is you can be a driver whenever you want or treat it like a regular job and make approximately $65,000 or more a year.

Wondering where you'll find paying customers? It's all in the mobile app which you can download and check out now. For more information visit:

Uber (Available in most major cities)

Lyft (Just like Uber but with a cute pink moustache)

Side.cr (Can set own price)

Shuddle.us (Community drivers for families)

If you don't have a car to drive and located in the California cities San

Francisco & San Jose, then you can rent out a car:

Joinbreeze ($50 a day which is cheaper than Enterprise which on average can be $70 a day to rent. Joinbreeze will also be expanding nationwide soon)

Here are two we covered earlier. The difference between these and joinbreeze are you'll be paying different fees. Try finding under $50 so you save starting out:

Relayrides

Getaround

9. Tutoring – school tutors are always in demand. Did you know that tutors can easily make $30 an hour and up? A little over 30 hours makes you $1,000.

My buddy tutored as a high-school student and I also tutored friends in my early twenties. Both times it gave me a feeling of importance and validation.

The money wasn't bad either. There are so many people (children and adults) that need tutoring. It's really one of my favorite things to do. I call it

Paid Volunteer Work ☐

Here's a start:

Instaedu

Tutor

Thumbtack

10. Teaching English/Other Languages – You probably take the fact that you speak English or another language fluently for granted.

At $20-$50 an hour you can literally open your mouth and make money. It's that simple.

English is a second language for many people. For some, it's a third, fourth, or even fifth language. There are so many nuances to English that it's very difficult to learn them via textbook and/or software. These people need a deeper understanding and you can provide it for them.

You can get certified to teach English as a foreign/second language (TEFL/

TESL). It'll cost you but you'll be able to go abroad or domestically teach

English.

There's always just posting an ad on Craigslist that you're willing to help.

Another option is trying:

Italki.com (Can set own rates and teach other languages)

Care

Thumbtack

11. Teaching music – what instrument can you play? Even if you have a basic understanding of music and the instrument, you can get paid for teaching those basics to people who want to learn.

You can also teach young novices. However, the parents are usually looking for someone very accomplished so their children can be the next

Beethoven or something like that.

Your ideal clients will be senior citizens. Head down to your nearest Senior Center and pass out flyers. Let's not forget this place to check for clients:

Thumbtack

12. Refereeing – You've been to a sports game of some sort for children, right? Hockey, soccer, football, basketball, tennis, etc. Have you seen the people who wear the striped shirts and blow the whistles every so often? You could be one of them.

If you're knowledgeable about a particular sport, you can apply for a referee position at your local park and/or recreation center. These referees make hundreds of dollars for a very short season making judgment calls for children's sporting events.

If refereeing isn't your thing there's always personal coaching. Check this out:

Coachup

13. Software Training – do you have any idea how many people install software that they have no idea how to use? Microsoft Office is one of the most popular software packages of all-time and millions of people could use your help with just the basics. You can show them in the comfort of your own home by just sharing computer screens using Skype, Join.me, or Screenhero. If you find that people are not savvy enough to use these than try this browser based video/screen share: Appear.in.

You can offer to install Microsoft Office or any program you notice which has a lot of trouble understanding and provide basic training for the tool suite. Here's a resource to try but you'll need to be certified:

Wesolved (Earn up to $50 an hour solving user's software issues)

14. Computer Setup – you have some basic computer skills, don't you? You'd be surprised how many people are intimidated by setting up their computers for the first time. Get out there and help these people. You can easily get $40 or $50 for doing this just one time.

Twenty more sessions and you'll have $1,000.

People will pay you for setting up simple stuff like anti-virus, email services, and passwords. You can *definitely* do this.

15. Bookkeeping – do you have bookkeeping skills? Are you proficient with QuickBooks or any other accounting software? Put a flyer up or try craigslist.

Bonus Tip: One-time jobs are great but ongoing weekly, monthly, and quarterly jobs are MUCH better. Once you get the gig see if you can turn it into a long term job.

16. Writing blog posts – There are more than a few blogs that you follow. How much have you learned from reading, liking, commenting, and sharing this information? Quite a bit, I bet. Well, if you enjoy it you should offer to write articles for them.

You don't have to be a literary giant. Your thoughts are your thoughts and they're valuable. Treat them as such. You should get about 25 bucks per article which can take roughly 30 minutes to research and 30 minutes to write. If you write 40, you've got $1,000. BAM – just like that! This is like working a 40 hour work week while staying in the comforts of home.

Here's one source where on average writers can make $30 a short blog post and $65 a long blog post:

Scripted

You can find more options here:

Elance

Odesk

Guru

Freelancer

17. Freelance editor/translator – Are you passionate about writing/editing or studied English/journalism? Can you translate English into a foreign language or vice versa? If so, you've got the skills necessary to edit and/or proofread documents for a fee.

You don't have to be a "professional" editor. You can find this type of work on Craigslist all day every day.

Remember, a few items back when we talked about bookkeeping? We said

"One-time jobs are great but ongoing weekly, monthly, and quarterly jobs are MUCH better." That applies here too.

You want to start thinking a little more long-term than just one-time jobs.

People don't need help just one-time. They're looking for an ongoing relationship. Give that to them and you're golden.

Tip: Email startups (aka new businesses) if they'd like to translate their entire pages into a foreign language in order to compete in global markets.

Just offer them a project fee and you can make your $1,000 fast. Find these startups here:

Betalis t

Producthun t

Erlibird

Here are three great freelance sources which have online marketplaces of buyers and sellers for editing/translating:

Elance

Odesk

Thumbtack

Guru

Freelancer

18. Office coordination – There are millions of people with home offices who need your help getting organized. And it's not just home offices, regular day-job corporate offices need your help too.

Lots of successful people have no idea how to organize their workspace.

They run around all day in what I like to call "organized confusion" and create little systems in their head for how their office should look even though it's not even close to the vision they have in mind. Lost documents and other important materials cost these business owners tons of money.

You would be doing these people a HUGE favor by arranging their offices for them. Put some flyers up around businesses or call using the yellow pages.

Oh yeah, and the pricing... After a few clients easily $1,000 a pop.

For office organizing:

Handybook

19. Simple mechanic work – you don't have to be ASE certified in order to work on someone's car; however it does increase trust with clients. If you can change belts, hoses, spark plugs, brakes, change oil, batteries and other simple stuff, you can make LOADS of cash.

This works best if you can travel to clients' homes or places of business to help them. Remember, people PAY for convenience.

Think about how appreciative you would be if you called someone up because you were having car trouble and they came to your home or place of business to fix your car.

Wouldn't you be pleased? Of course you would. And you would PAY EXTRA for that type of convenience wouldn't you? Yes. You would. Other people will too. Put some flyers, ask around the neighborhood, or a

Facebook/Tweet out so you can get hired or try these websites:

Handybook (Make $45 an hour as a handyman)

Thumbtack

20. Medical claims – every single day people deal with surgery and illnesses. Did you know you can get paid for helping someone with their medical claims?

You have to know the ropes for this one. If you've dealt with and filed claims with insurance companies, you can help people straighten out their situation and get things done quickly and easily. This is a MAJOR Service that people will PAY for. And again, you don't have to be certified or anything like that. All you need is a little bit of know-how.

21. Simple Website Setup – are you familiar with WordPress, CSS, HTML, and/or PHP? If so, you can easily get paid $250 a pop to set up simple websites. If you have no clue then you should educate yourself. Youtube.com has plenty of tutorials.

This is something I did for a couple weeks a few years back. I cleared $2,000 in 3 weeks. I charged $250 a pop. You can do this. *As little as you think you know right now, somebody knows even less* and you would be an absolute savior to them. I can speak from experience when I tell you that this one flat-out works!

22. Organizing tax records – This one is a little more involved than simple book keeping. If you've got administrative skills and are familiar with tax forms and/or software, you may be able to offer your services to someone who needs help preparing their paperwork and organizing it.

We all know that tax season ends on April 15th. However, there are very many people who extend it all the way to October 15th. Those are the people who need your help the most.

23. Social Media Director – if you're well-versed in all things social, you can DEFINITELY make $1,000 quickly. Quite honestly, you can make a side business or even a career from utilizing this skillset to serve others.

Businesses are starting to understand the value of social media more and more every day. Gone are the days of Yellow Pages and newspaper ads.

Today, EVERYTHING is social. As a matter of fact, for many consumers, if you don't have a social media presence, they won't even do business with you.

Facebook, Twitter, Google Plus, YouTube, FourSquare, LivingSocial, Groupon etc. are outlets that businesses are looking to be present on. Help them get the word out about their business and watch how quickly your life changes. Just find a local business and ask if they want someone to help them on social media then give them a price for that service.

24. Professional House Stager – do you watch HGTV? If so, you know exactly what it takes to stage a home. If you can make a home look like it belongs in a showcase, then you can do this.

You don't even have to watch HGTV (it helps but it's not necessary). If you have a passion for interior decoration and design, then this could work perfectly for you. Doubly so, if you're attending classes for these subjects. It would be like paid training. Technically, it is.

Bonus Tip: Real estate agents will be your absolute BEST clients for this service. And the best part? They're easy to find. Any free magazine in a supermarket or search engine will find you hundreds of potential clients.

Work for a discount or even for free on a trial basis. If you're good, you'll make all the money back from your free/discounted session and then some.

25. Event Planner – have you ever been to a party and said to yourself "I wish I had planned this party, it would be WAY better" If so, you can be an event planner.

This works best if you have a group of friends that party with you and know, like, and trust you. These will be your very best advocates. They'll use word-of-mouth marketing to spread the word like wildfire.

My aunt is an event planner. She started her business 20 years ago doing exactly what I'm telling you that you can do. If you've got work ethic, people skills, and love to party, this is a GOLDMINE for you.

A friend of mine in college used to hold business and charity events at bars. He'd call the bars ahead of time and work out a price he could make off the top for everyone he'd bring through the door.

That month he'd hype up the event around campus, on Facebook, twitter and then have these people meet him there. Needless to say after a few events he raked in $2,000 partnering with the bars.

It doesn't just have to be bars for you. You could be the middle man for any place that can host a large event and collect money just for organizing it.

Some helpful services to get you started:

Squadup

Meetup

Eventbrite

26. Affiliate Marketing – It's a simple concept. Find something you really like, tell people about it, give them a website link to purchase, and take a cut of the money. It's really that easy!

Anyone and everyone that has any type of product or service are ALWAYS looking for people to sell their products and services for them. Remember, you're solving a problem. These people are BUSY. They don't have time to promote their business. They barely have time to run it and live a "normal" life. Reach out to them and ask if you can help them sell their products and services.

In the online world, this is as easy as a few mouse clicks. However, I want you to think outside the box. What kind of offline companies can you do this for? Hair salons, restaurants, chiropractors, dentists, etc. Negotiate a referral program and start selling.

27. Create and/or edit videos – creating videos are easy. You can do them in front of the camera or behind the camera and they both work just fine. Millions of businesses need videos created for them so they can put them on YouTube and their own company websites.

Help these people. They *NEED* you. This works well for ANY business. In case you haven't noticed, people don't read as much as they used to and their attention spans are dwindling down to nothing. If you can create engaging videos and/or edit some bad ones, then you can make money hand over fist.

My buddy started a business similar to this a few years ago. It's a business that fueled his growth as an entrepreneur and helped him become a homeowner in less than a year. All it takes is a little know-how and some hustle. Businesses NEED this service. Get out there and help them. Editing projects go for $1,000-$4,000.

If you're making animations try these simple drag and drop programs:

Goanimate (Starts at $39 a month to use)

Powtoon (Starts at $0-$19)

Videoscribe (Starts at $29 a month)

Explee (Starts at $7 a month)

Animaker (Launching soon)

If you have no experience for creating videos try making some samples or doing it for free/cheap. Just remind these companies that you'll be saving them time and money. Mention how you're studying this and enthusiastic about it. They may give you a shot. If they like your work ask for a testimonial and referral.

Another idea is package deals: Once you get good or just starting out find a good company that has no website or video. Don't forget owners of crappy sites too.

Ask if they want a better one. Offer to do it all for $1,000. Just study for a few days or watch some Youtube tutorials.

I'm sure there's probably a 10 year old showing how to build a fast website without coding on youtube or sign up with wix, squarespace, or weebly.

They're simple drag and drop website builders. It's like playing with Legos.

Also since these companies charge monthly you should charge these businesses monthly to manage their company websites.

Imagine managing 10 sites for $100 a month. That's $1,000 of reoccurring revenue every month! And it doesn't stop there! Build more sites for people, charge for custom logos and if you're good at design, and you can get up to $10,000 a month of maintenance. I knew a guy who used this exact business model. He dropped out of college and hired an offshore team to help him scale to higher monthly amounts.

You're probably thinking why would these people hire you if they can figure it out themselves? The truth is anyone can but all this takes time, patience, and interest to solve this problem. Plus most people still believe creating well designed websites are hard or would rather spend more important parts of their business elsewhere. If you can take the stress away so they sleep like a baby at night they'll gladly pay you.

If you're just doing videos try these…

Get customers on:

Elance

Odesk

Freelancer

Guru

Pitch at startups which you can find at:

Producthun t

Betalis t

Erlibird

28. Bargain Hunter – we all know that in order to make a profit, we need to buy low and sell high. Well, if you have an eye for bargains and frequent thrift stores, flea markets, and garage sales, then you can make quite a bit of money.

You can find fantastic deals at garage sales and then come home, hop on your computer, and sell the same items you just purchased for double, triple, and even quadruple what you paid for them.

Have you ever watched the TV show Storage Wars? If so, you know that people come in and buy the contents of delinquent storage containers and then sell that stuff to people and/or places willing to pay more than what they paid for it. Can you do this? Yes. You. Can.

I also remember helping a buddy of mine in college who started out this way. We would load up his pickup truck with used furniture he'd find around the city off Craigslist. He paid for my help in free lunch for a week.

Then he'd take the furniture back home, fix them up till they looked brand new, took nice photos, and then sold them for triple back on craigslist. Now there's more websites you can sell on; I'll share them later in this guide.

In 2 weeks, he had $3,500 and a huge smile on his face. That was then and now which is 8 years later he's opening his second furniture store with the same type of business in mind.

29. Research Papers – research is easier than it has ever been.

However, there are people who simply refuse to do it and/or don't have the time to do it themselves. Find those people and offer your services to them.

By searching Craigslist and putting flyers in local colleges, you'll find more clients than you can handle.

All you need is a knack for research. The rest takes care of itself. Just name your price and see if they hook. Besides

elance & **odesk** you can also try:

Writeraccess

Scripted

30. Voiceover – there's a chance your voice is the type someone is looking for in their online or radio commercial. You'll never know until you try. So find a quiet room away from distraction, stand up to project your voice, and record some samples.

You don't need the most professional equipment right now. Just use your mobile phone or computer microphone. Try these websites for voiceover work:

Voicebunny

Voices

31. Lobby politicians – With multiple interests out there it's tough for groups to get their needs met. So to push causes they've looked to hire normal people such as you and I. You don't have to be an expert talker just someone passionate about movements. Here's a service where you can contact congress representatives and work as a personal lobbyist:

Amplifyd (Make $12-$30 an hour)

Chapter 3
Medical Community Participation

Participating in the medical community is a great way to earn extra cash.

Remember how we talked about using your house to make money? Well, in this instance you can actually "use your body" to make money.

Your organs, tissue, bones, cartilage, etc. is insanely valuable. There are people on life support right now that need all sorts of human body parts.

If we lived in a true free market economy, your body would be worth a lot of money. Your organs would be the most valuable. Items like your heart, lungs, kidneys, pancreas, etc. If you went out and sold your kidney as opposed to simply donating it, then it would go to the highest bidder that was a match for your kidney.

However, the US government (and other countries) don't allow this sort of thing.

Let's take a look at a few of the ways you can use your body to make money legally.

32. Sell plasma – This is slightly different than selling blood.

There are fluids and tiny bits that circulate through your blood system.

That's what you're actually selling.

Here's how the process works…

First, you find the nearest plasma donation center. Then you go up to the desk and give them your identification.

First timers will be required to take a physical examination. You'll give them a blood sample from your finger and then fill out a donor questionnaire.

If you're eligible to donate, the technician will prepare your arm and begin the process. As blood is drawn, there's a separation process that takes place. Plasma is separated from your blood and red blood cells will be returned to your body.

This process takes about 2 hours the first time around and 90 minutes thereafter. When you're done you check out and get paid. It's that simple.

Be aware that there is no set compensation for your donation. The amount you get paid is determined by each plasma collection facility.

Try this resource for plasma:

Donatingplasma

33. Sell your hair – Hairy people (also called hirsute) can make some quick cash by selling off their hair. Generally speaking, hair should be at least 10 inches long and naturally colored (no fancy dyes)

I grew up around women. One thing I know for sure is that they pay (and pay well) to have their hair done. Women do all sorts of things to their hair that requires them to have extra hair added so they can have the style that they want. Hair is big business. And of course, I'm not being sexist, men can sell their hair too.

Some people grow their hair long for 5, 10, or 20 years and then make a decision to cut it all off and start from scratch. Next time you think about cutting your hair and you've been growing it for a long time, think about how you might be able to sell it instead of your hairstylist sweeping it into the trash can.

For those people that take really good care of their hair, your "donation" will be worth even more. Buyers don't want over-shampooed and/or sun damaged hair.

These are useful place for people looking to buy and sell real human hair:

OnlineHairAffair

Hairsellon

34. Sell breast milk – Some mothers find themselves with an overabundance of breast milk. This milk can be sold on the internet.

Please keep in mind that this is of questionable legality and could potentially have some health issues. It's kind of like a *black market* sort of thing. Because of its potentially legal issues, we can't recommend it.

However, I did want to offer it as a solution because it's not illegal all over the world; just in some places.

Try looking here:

Onlythebreast

Mothersmilk

Nationalmilkbank

35. Sell Sperm – There are those out there that need our help in bringing a child into this world. However, there are some prerequisites such as a certain height, health or ethnicity sought after. Men can make $30-$100 per sperm donation and choose to remain anonymous.

Here are some of the resources:

Spermbankdirectory (A list of places you can call and ask for compensation)

Spermbank (Multiple locations & $100 every time you donate)

36. Sell Eggs – Having a baby isn't always easy for heterosexual or homosexual couples. Sometimes they need outside assistance.

Prerequisites to donate apply and you also have the ability to remain anonymous.
Women can make up to $5,000-$10,000!

You'll want to investigate some of these:

Thedonorsource (Only in major cities around the US)

Circleeggdonation (Only available in Boston, Denver, Los Angeles, North Carolina, and Oregon)

37. Become a surrogate – If you're a healthy woman you have the opportunity of having a couple's baby. This entails first interviewing to meet your couple match, insemination, and then carrying their baby for 9 months till you deliver. Risks are involved and you should contact your doctor before you decide to embark on this journey.

Surrogate mothers are paid on average $25,000 to $50,000.

Check out these resources:

Thesurrogacysource

Circlesurrogacy

38. Participate in medical studies – The medical community is always testing and trying out new things for the betterment of humanity. They pay people to participate in medical trials. All you need to be is a healthy adult and test a drug. Note: There can always be a chance of drug side effects when risking your health. You should think wisely or consult your doctor beforehand. However, if you do choose to participate then *you can make $1,000-$7,000 from one study!*

Do your research in following sources and apply:

Centerwatch

Testwiththebest (Limited locations)

Newhavencru (Limited to Connecticut)

Clinicalconnection (Most of these studies are only available if you already have a health issue rather than for healthy volunteers)

Biotrax (Limited locations & you'll need to call to find out compensation amount)

Chapter 4
Get A Grip On Your Spending Habits

I already know what you're thinking… "I'm pushed to the limit. Everything I spend money on is a necessity." Let me just call that excuse what it is right now…

It's B.S. and you know it!

Remember the pep talk from Chapter 2? Well, here comes another one.

You're in a cash crunch because either something unexpected happened that you absolutely had to spend money on. Or you simply ran out of money because you spent your money on stuff that really doesn't matter.

Now of course, what I say doesn't matter and what you say doesn't matter are two completely different things. I get that. But ask yourself…

"Did I really need to go out to dinners, movies, clubs, sporting events, vacations, etc. as much as I did?"

And if you're being truthful, the answer is NO.

Look, I'm all about having fun. Life is meant to be enjoyed. Party as hard as you want. Enjoy life to the fullest. But don't be silly and blow your money and then put yourself in a pinch because you were too busy "living it up" with friends to take care of what needs to be taken care of.

There is an abundance of money out there. You might not believe it. But it's absolutely true. All you have to do is provide a service to someone and you'll make money. It's really that simple.

However, this chapter is about changing your spending habits. It's something you'll need to do for at least a short period of time to get your life back in order. And who knows? Maybe you'll get the hang of it and start doing it long term so you can have more fun with your leftover money.

Here are a few things you can do starting today…

39. Eat cheaper food – you probably spend quite a bit of money at the grocery store. Most of us do. However, try going on a pinto/black beans and healthy meat (skinless chicken, turkey, tuna, or beef) diet for a week or month.

Maybe eating only beans and meat for a week won't work for you. If you spend $200 per week in groceries, you can easily cut that in half by focusing on only low cost foods. Pasta, potatoes, salads and other stuff is very low cost and if you only eat cheap food for a little while, you'll start to notice that your wallet or purse is heavier than it used to be.

There's also cooking most of your meals on certain days of the week then storing them in Tupperware. This is to fend off any laziness you may feel by going out and spending unnecessary money. You don't need that pizza or burger. All you'll need to do is reheat your premade food and dig in.

When I was a young kid (about 7 years old), my parents started the delicate and smart art of couponing. Just grab that supermarket mail you would have thrown away and see what's on sale.

Another weird hack is using smaller plates and eating slower. Perhaps, finishing everything on our plate comes from when mom and dad yelled at us as kids. At least we can use this old habit by finishing everything on a smaller plate. I also recommend drinking a tall glass of water with each meal to hydrate yourself and make you feel fuller. This will save you cash, make you healthy, and you'll even avoid that dreaded food coma.

40. Eat Out Less – how often do you eat out? Probably more than you want to admit. Reduce it right now. I'm serious.

A dinner for two at a place like Applebee's or Olive Garden will typically cost about $50 when you include tax and tip. If you eat out once or twice a week, you could easily put that money back in your pocket and use it towards other things.

I'll admit that this one is tough. Primarily because eating out is usually an occasion for couples. It is most often paired with a night at the movies or visiting a comedy club. Date night is very important if you're going to keep your romantic relationship alive. However, in a cash crunch, you will more than likely have to cut back for a little while. Try cooking for each other followed by watching a movie comfortably at home. Search "free event" on here and see what you find:

Yelp

There's another rub to this as well. For busy families with children it's tough to come home after 5PM and still cook something for the children to eat.

"Dominos and McDonalds are on the way home from soccer practice.

Which one would you like kids?"

This question is asked over and over again in busy families. If you're in a cash crunch this has to be reduced immediately.

"But you don't understand… I'm busy."

Everyone is busy. You must find a way to eat at home. How about stopping by the grocery store before you go home instead of the drive-thru?

Again, I know you might not like the sound of this. But in a cash crunch, you need to make some sacrifices.

To understand how much money you're losing eating out and other ways check out these safe apps:

Mint (Once you link your banking you'll get a monthly/chart on your spending)

Billguard (This one is similar to Mint but exclusively mobile and will let know as soon as purchase something. Great to catch fraud or set a monthly spending budget)

Eating out also includes that morning coffee you buy at your favorite café.

Even if it's a ritual for you imagine avoiding 2 weeks of it. Would that be enough to buy a cheap coffee maker and some beans you can roast at home?

"Oh, I just don't have time in the morning to brew my coffee!"

If you can walk or drive to a café then you do have time. Quit being lazy and set the coffee maker the night before so when you wake up all you need to do is push a button for instant coffee.

41. Cut the cable– Cable costs $100 per month (typically).

You can save big, often $100 or more by simply shutting off your cable TV.

This one might be even tougher than not eating out. People like to come home, eat dinner, and then sit in front of the TV for a few hours before going to bed. That's the cycle for millions of people. Chances are you're one of them.

However, the TV isn't as important as it once was. As long as you have internet, you can watch whatever you want to watch. And on top of that, how many people do you know that still use a landline? Not many I bet.

Your cell phone is with you all the time. Why do you need a landline?

Realistically, you can cut cable and just keep internet and your cell phone and life will not end as you know it. You'll probably find that you're better off this way. Plus if you still crave entrainment there are many options:

Amazon Prime ($99 a year, $8.25 a month)

Netflix ($96 a year, $8 a month)

Hulu ($96 year, $8 a month)

42. Reduce "sinning" – this isn't a religious thing at all. When I mention the word "sin" what I really mean is a vice of some sort.

We all have a vice of some sort. Video games, cigarettes, and alcohol are all considered vices. Of course there's a ton more. Just think about how much money you would save if you cut back on this type of stuff for a month. You would be out of your cash crunch in no time.

Usually these activities involve spending our time and money with friends. If you need to save cash just let them know you're busy to hang out or be honest and tell them you're on a tight budget. Then offer to meet them at some of the free events we discussed earlier.

However, if you're finding battling your vices too difficult then we recommend this web browser extension. At least you can discovery deals for things you'd normally purchase and save hundreds at the end of the month:

Shopgeniusapp

Chapter 5
Micro Projects

I consider micro projects the Holy Grail of making money in real life and online. It's so easy to get started and there's instant gratification. It also goes right back to the beginning when I talked about providing services and solving problems.

Micro projects don't pay very much per task ($5-$20). But if you do enough of them, the cash stacks up pretty quickly. I'm going to give you more than a dozen websites that you can go to right this minute and start earning money.

43. Gigwalk – if you can take photos, pick up menus, and do other small tasks while you're walking around throughout the day, then this is just the site for you.

What I love about Gigwalk is its completely mobile. All you have to do is go to the website, enter your cell phone number, download an app and start doing assignments. You get paid via PayPal.

Although this is open to everybody, it's important to maintain professionalism and courtesy. Your work is scored and the higher you score, the more complex the jobs become and the more money you can make. You can even land a full-time position with some of these companies if you so choose. Or maybe even strike up some sort of partnership.

44. Mechanical Turk – This is Amazon's work from home assignment program. Small tasks like writing reviews and editing documents is the norm.

This one is very simple as well. Some tasks pay very little and some pay more. Note: When you click find HITs, look for the box that says "that pay at least" and type in an amount $10-$40 to find high paying tasks.

It's all dependent on what you can handle. It's very data-driven. So if you perform tasks well, you'll be able to take on more complex tasks and get paid a little more.

Sometimes you have to prove your eligibility for a particular task by participating in an exam of some sort. It's only fair that people paying you to do something make sure that you can actually do it before you waste their time and yours. Don't be put off by this. Just work within the system and everything will be okay.

45. TaskRabbit – This one is very similar to Gigwalk. The primary difference is that it's limited to just a few cities. They also do background checks.

Running quick deliveries and doing office assignments is very common on Task Rabbit. You browse open tasks, find something that interests you, and then make an offer telling the "employer" how much money you expect to make for completing the task.

Keep in mind that other people will be bidding against you. Don't sell yourself short. Just be mindful that you're not the only person who is aiming for that particular task. Top earners who recommend focusing on getting good in one task are making $1,500 a week.

46. FOAP – these guys offer smartphone users and photographers the opportunity to earn money from their photos. You'll collect $5 every time your photo is sold.

You know those selfies that you take all the time? Well, they're worth money. Over at FOAP you simply download their free app, snap a few photos, and upload them to the FOAP market.

Someone will buy your photo and then you'll get paid. The best part is that you can sell the same photo to different people (or even the same person) over and over again. This is a great way to get paid.

47. MobileWorks – these guys are changing the way the world works. They're reinventing traditional outsourcing.

MobileWorks teaches individuals from countries all over the world how to participate in the online economy. They provide businesses a socially responsible way to get work done. They use a product by the name of Lead

Genius that helps businesses grow by finding new leads for them. This is a great way to earn extra money.

Similar to mobileworks, Fancyhands allows busy people to hire virtual assistants. The work is task based on finding hotel deals, booking a plane try trip, data entry or scheduling appointments. Task pay: $2.50-$7.

Fancyhands.com

48. WeGoLook – this one is self-explanatory. What you do is verify and inspect things on behalf of businesses.

You'll inspect buildings, cars, boats, homes, and other high value items.

You make sure it works. You take some snapshots and you fill out any forms provided to you by the businesses.

You will need to pass a background check for this one. Also, you get paid in

2-4 weeks, not instantly. That could be a drawback for some. However, this is a great way to earn money. You can receive $25 per inspection.

49. Fiverr – this is where a lot of people get started (myself included). You post simple tasks on the site and get paid $5 per job.

The kind of work you do on Fiverr varies. There's a ton of categories. You can do something like video creation, email writing, repair websites, and the list goes on and on. Look at what gigs have the most buyers and go from there.

You're not limited to $5. That's just a starting point. More work will require more gigs which will earn you more money.

Let's say you're doing video creation. For $5 you might offer a 30 second video. If the client wants a longer video of say 2 minutes, then you would charge them accordingly. Instead of making $5, you'd make $20.

For lots of great tips on getting the most from Fiver check out FIVERRPOWERTIPS.COM

50. AgentAnything – run errands, do temp work, and do some light marketing and you'll make money. The tasks are actually called "missions". It sounds cooler than task and gives you a feeling of adventure.

This one is mostly for college students but anyone can do this. Stuff like holding someone's place in line, packing, and picking up flowers is very commonplace.

Note: Only available in New York & New Jersey but expanding other places.

51. User Testing – this is one of the fastest ways for businesses to get feedback about their products. You simply review websites, products, and services and give real-time feedback.

Website owners pay to watch you review their site. You use the screen recorder from UserTesting to record a video of what's happening on your screen. Answer four simple questions about your experience. Then you get paid $10 via PayPal.

Your face is not recorded. This doesn't require a webcam or any sort of special software.

52. MiNeeds – you compete for jobs with this one. It's kind of like thumbtack, taskrabbit, and handybook. People who need services like accountants, photographers, nannies and dentists post their needs and then you compete for that job. It doesn't just stop at those 3 services there's at least 40 more. Take a look and see what you can provide.

This is a great way for someone with a defined set of skills to earn extra money. It's also great for small businesses that need more customers.

Chapter 6
Squeeze More Cash Out Of Your Job

You're not confined to your salary or hourly wage at work. You have to think outside of the box, but you can definitely make some extra cash at work.

53. Volunteer for overtime – It's very likely that extra hours are available at your job. Your job might be a drag and you might hate it.

But if you're in a cash crunch, let your supervisor know that you're available for extra work.

54. Take on the "ugly" work – If overtime isn't available, here's another option; There are tasks and jobs within your company that nobody else wants. Offer to do them and watch your stock rise. If possible, negotiate to get paid for this extra work outside of your normal paycheck.

55. Employee referral program – turnover is inevitable and costly within companies. Your friends and/or family might be the perfect fit for an open position at your company. Ask your employer if they have a program like this. If so, start referring people. This is EASY money

56. Customer referral program – every company spends tons of time and money searching for customers. What if you were able to bring in a few customers to your company? You'd be seen as a hero.

Who knows, you might even get a promotion!

57. Make a useful suggestion – your company probably has a suggestion box. Most employees completely bypass it. Put your thinking cap on and figure out a way for your company to grow revenue, cut expenses, or improve processes. You'll get a bonus and some recognition.

Chapter 7
Quick Cash From Moonlighting

Of course you can make some quick cash off the job as well. Maybe you don't even want to be bothered with trying to make extra cash at your day job because you already spend too much time there and don't like the job anyway. That's entirely understandable. Here's a few ways for you to make some quick cash after hours.

58. Babysitting – if you're great with children and have some extra time, this is a great way to make some extra cash. Most of the time you'll get paid $10-25 an hour or more. Try these resources to find customers:

Caretango

Care

Sittercity

Mineeds

Teacherr Earn up to $30+ per hour in the US. Some benefits include live in accommodation, weekend Hampton trips or Yacht trips in the Bahamas

59. Pet sitting – this is very similar to babysitting but with less hassle for the most part. Taking care of a pet doesn't require constant care. All you have to do is feed, walk, make sure doggy/kitty doesn't ruin anything in the house, and you're good to go.

Because pet sitting is so simple and requires so little, it's very easy to maintain several pet sitting jobs at one time. Here's a service to sign up with:

Holidog

Worthee

In the same category there's dog walking. Here's one available only in New York City. Dog walkers can make $12-15 per duration. You can always borrow the idea and contact dog owners around your city:

Swifto

60. House sitting – some people are simply never home because they're always travelling for business and/or pleasure. These people need someone trustworthy to housesit for them. It doesn't require much. Just pop in once or twice a day and make sure there's nothing weird going on or stay home and watch their pets.

Note: In order for these websites to deliver content and continue running they may charge an annual fee. To overcome this you'll need to advertise in your profile how much you'll charge to maintain homes while homeowners are away.

Nomador

Trustedhousesitters

Housesittersamerica

61. Temp jobs – These are available during the summer and the holidays. During those peak times, companies are slammed with business and need extra employees.

Try this website:

Indeed.com

62. Deliver goods – There's a lot of busy and lazy people out there that need certain things. This is kind of like taskrabbit and gigwalk but based around making deliveries. Some need food; some need their clothing while others need grocery shopping done. The following companies allow you to help these people while making money.

Getwashio Deliver wash and folded clothing. Only available in San Francisco, Los Angeles, and Washington DC

Instacart Deliver and shop for groceries for $25 an hour. Available in certain areas of: Atlanta, Austin, Boston, Chicago, Denver, Los Angeles, New York City, Philadelphia, San Francisco Bay Area, Seattle, and Washington, D.C.

Doordash Deliver food and make $20 an hour. Only Available in

California for now

Postmates Deliver food and make $20 an hour. Available in San

Francisco, New York City, DC, Chicago, Seattle, many more coming soon)

Rinse Deliver and inspect laundry. Only available in San Francisco

Sprig Deliver food. Only available in San Francisco

Trycaviar Deliver food from top restaurants to people's homes and offices. Make $10/ Delivery+ 5% of the order total. Available in major cities

Taskrabbit Deliver anything requested

Wunwun Deliver anything requested and make about $20 per delivery. Only available in New York City and Hamptons

63. Referral agent for salespeople – real estate agents, insurance agents, and car salespeople are always on the hunt for more clients. Help these people out by referring business to them and they'll be very grateful. Since these sales are worth quite a bit of money to these agents, getting $100 for referring a sale is relatively simple.

64. Personal Stylist – If you have an eye for style then how about becoming a personal stylist? There are plenty of people who would love your expertise. As a stylist you can make $40-90 an hr. After 11-25 hours that's $1,000.

Here's a website where you can apply and get customers:

Sharesomestyle

65. Photographer – Photographers pricing is out of control. They charge quite a bit of money to do work that you can do just as well for a lot less. If you're good at photography, go out and shoot a special event.

Someone will pay you $300 (or more). Another way is to upload your pictures to websites which will pay you:

Shutterstock

Crated

Istockphoto

Photodune (You can get paid for a few other digital things on here)

66. Gym Instructor – you don't have to be a personal trainer to work at the gym. Most gyms offer several different types of classes.

Yoga, Zumba, and indoor cycling are just a few of them. Chances are there's a position waiting for you at your local gym. Head over there and find out how you can be of assistance.

Joinvint Only available in SF and you can make $20 a workout session or more depending on what you choose to set

67. Product reviews – do you buy lots of electronics? Are you always testing out new stuff? If so, you can very easily write product reviews for popular blogs. These blogs usually have affiliate arrangements with big manufacturers. They'll pay you to review items that you buy anyway.

A creative way people have done this is signing up to youtube.com's partner program. They make videos and every time someone views the ads or clicks you make some money. A few change here and there will add up at the end of the week.

68. Bartender – do you know your way around the bar? Are you familiar with the most popular drinks? Do you like to party? If so, bartending is a great way to make some extra cash. Check craigslist or post what you can do for someone.

Remember, you don't have to work in a bar or a club. You can do weekend parties and weddings and pull in an easy $100 (or more) per party. Here's a few sites to post your bartending skills:

Gigsalad

Thumbtack

69. Focus groups – focus groups are a demographically diverse group of people assembled to participate in a discussion about a particular product or service. These people get paid to simply offer their opinion. Colleges in your local area and Craigslist are a great way to find these types of opportunities.

Note: If certain focus groups or surveys want you to buy something first to participate don't do that study. It's likely that task will take months to get paid.

Pktesting

Influencerresearchpanel (You can earn $75-$250 per 2 hour session)

Findfocusgroups

70. Session musician – You can work as a "session" musician by getting paid only when you work within the band or orchestra. Bands and orchestras come in all sizes. If you can play an instrument, you can make money as a musician. It's not as difficult as some people make it out to be.

Gigsalad

Craigslist

71. Moving Billboard – most standard billboards are being replaced by digital boards that rotate advertisements. But even those aren't as effective as having a billboard on your car or truck.

Everywhere you go, the message will be seen. Even when you're in a parking lot, people still see your message. Call some mom and pop shops up that aren't too big and see if they'd pay for you to advertise them.

Here's one service that's going nationwide:

Advercar You can make up to $100 a month with this one!

Iwearyourshirt A t-shirt company where you can get paid to wear shirts. They may not be currently looking for walking billboard but you can always sign up

72. Moving furniture – many people have figured out that you don't need a professional moving company to help you move. These are the people you can help by moving furniture for them. This works well with Craigslist. Sometimes people post looking for extra help from "non-professionals". And you can also post to Craigslist yourself advertising that you're willing to help people move.

Buddytruk (Only available in Los Angeles but expanding soon.

Make $40 an hour helping people move or haul stuff)

Getbellhops (Only open to college students can make $12-$15 an hour)

Tryhousecall

Taskrabbit

73. Cutting lawns – a few months ago I had a young man who couldn't have been more than 15 years old come by my house and cut my grass for only $15. I didn't feel like doing it so I paid him. He didn't place any fancy advertisement. He just saw that my grass was long, knocked on the door, and asked if I would like him to cut it. You can do the same thing around your neighborhood or try:

Taskrabbit

74. Painting – Painting is easy. All you need is a few supplies and some time and you're good to go. People ALWAYS need paint done and most would prefer not to pay the high prices of professionals.

Help these people out and paint for them. $150 per room is very reasonable. Here's a few sites to find gigs:

Paintzen

Tryhousecall

Handybook Make up to $45 an hour as a handyman

75. Shoveling Snow – As a kid, my buddy loved doing this. He made $100 every time it snowed. You can do this too. There's no age limit or anything like that. All you need is a shovel and some hustle and you're good to go.

76. Cleaning Houses – as mentioned before, people are busy.

They don't have time to clean their houses thoroughly. They try to keep it neat and tidy but very often life gets in the way and the house becomes a mess. You should be able to make at least $100 by cleaning a house top to bottom.

Zaarly Only available in San Francisco, California and Kansas City, Kansas

Handybook Make up to $22/hour as a cleaner or $45/hour as a handyman

Homejoy Make $12-$15 plus tips

Tryhousecall Set your own amount per service

Thumbtack Set your own amount per service

77. Washing and detailing cars – I'm not the type of person that likes to clean cars but maybe you are. You can make some easy money by doing something you like that other people dislike.

Washing a car is one thing. If you can "detail" a car you should be able to make $100 fairly quickly or to find customers try:

Tryhousecall

Wype (Launching soon in California. You can make $12-$35 an hour)

78. Cleaning gutters – if you're not afraid of heights, this can work for you. All you need to do is climb a ladder, get some basic supplies and clear the gutters of debris. Tell your neighbors what you're offering to do or put some flyers up.

79. Pool setup – people that have pools don't really know much about the technical aspects of them. And very rarely do they attempt to set them up themselves. Also, when the colder weather comes and

it's time to shut the pool down, the same people who called you to set it up will likely be the same people to call you to shut it down.

Set your own amount per service:

Tryhousecal l

Thumbtack

80. Holiday decorations – I love the holidays. But I hate setting up the decorations. I've paid people to setup Easter, Halloween,

Thanksgiving, and Christmas decorations in the past. There are millions of people just like me. Put up an ad during holiday times and watch what happens.

81. Taking surveys – this is similar to the focus group but it's on an individual basis. Companies pay for opinions because they use that data to create better products and services. You receive points which then can be redeemed for money and gift cards.

Here are some options:

Opinionoutpost

I-say

MySurvey

Cashcrate

Globaltestmarket

82. Mystery shopper – You'll be working with several companies to improve the customer service metrics. Here's where you can find a job board for assignments:

MSPA (Pays from $17 to $150)

83. Marketing research – in this instance you're not conducting the research. You're simply participating. Companies are always performing market research.

Sign up with: Concepts Consumer Research (Participants can receive $20 to $1000 for performing product evaluations)

84. Clean carpets – there are millions of people who need their carpets cleaned. They know they can go rent or buy a machine and do it themselves; but most people don't want to. So, you go out and rent the machine and do it for them.

Here's a source of customers:

Tryhousecal l

85. Chef – Turns out people love to try new things especially food for the group of people calling themselves "foodies." This could be the start of your food blogging business or just networking with open people. Here's a service that allows you to host and charge for meals.

Eatfeastly You can set the price at $0-$250

86. Personal Servant – For males only and only available in San

Francisco. This may seem like a joke but there's actually a market forming around this. You can make $80 an hour and about $300 a day from this:

Manservants

87. Sell or Rent your gym pass to local travelers – People are always traveling for leisure or for business. While out some like to maintain their fitness. This company allows you to sell your gym pass to guests for

$5 a day or higher when you're not using it. You can also set the price for a week or month. Five bucks isn't much but if you live in a major city that has tourists it can quickly add up; not only paying for your pass but making you profit.

Gymsurfing

Chapter 8
Sell Your Junk

Have you ever seen the TV Show "Hoarders"? If so, you know that people keep all kinds of junk that they don't even need. All of that stuff that is considered junk by some can be *sold for profit*. So not only do you make money, but you also de-clutter in the process.

Remember, one man's trash is another man's treasure. Here's a few ways for you to sell your junk.

88. Garage Sale – you don't even have to leave the house. Just go through your basement, attic, and closets and start pulling stuff out.

You'd be surprised how much money you make. $100 per garage sale is very common or try this if you'd rather ship it:

Chairish.com

Reqwip.com Cash out on your quality cycling, triathlon, outdoor, or sports equipment instead of forgetting about it in your closet

89. Craigslist.org – if you don't feel like hauling everything out of your house, you can sell it piece-by-piece on Craigslist. This is great for large items like tables, sofas, appliances and the like.

90. eBay.com – it's almost exactly like Craigslist. You don't have to leave the house and you can sell items piece-by-piece. eBay is great for selling smaller items that are rather unique.

91. Sell other people's stuff on Craigslist and eBay – Kick your eBay and Craigslist selling up a notch by selling other people's stuff.

Sometimes people just don't want to go through the hassle or the learning curve. Make it easy for them. Offer to sell their stuff for them and give them a cut.

You'll have an endless supply of stuff to sell forever and ever and have happy neighbors and friends.

92. Amazon – Just like eBay and Craigslist, you can sell stuff on Amazon. Books, music, and movies are the most common items to sell there.

93. Half.com – Evidently eBay got tired of Amazon hogging all the media and book sales. Half.com is a place to sell entertainment media and textbooks that is owned by eBay.

94. Resell Gift Cards – when people don't know what to buy you for holidays and birthdays, they usually give you gift cards. They're probably tucked away in your purse or wallet and haven't even been used.

You can sell these unused gift cards on *CardCash* or any of the websites I just listed. Since you're not using your gift cards, you might as well sell them. Don't expect full value. You won't get it. But it's better to have cash in your wallet instead of unused gift cards anyway.

95. Swap Meet/Flea Markets – this is just like a garage sale. The only difference is it's not at your house. You pack up all your junk and take it to these places where there's a lot more buyers for this kind of stuff.

96. Sell your old computers and mobile devices – Some of your used electronic equipment might have value. If you're the kind of person that replaces your stuff every 6-12 months, then you're sitting on a goldmine. Head over to Gazelle and find out what your stuff is worth.

97. Collect and sell scrap metal – my buddy's uncle did this for a long time as a side hustle and made some serious bank for a number of years. All you need is a light pick-up truck or a sturdy trailer and you're good to go. His uncle rode around the neighborhood looking for this stuff. When he found it, he would load it up in the truck and take it to the junkyard. They would give him *cash on the spot* and he would come home and help pay bills with it. It really is a timeless money maker.

98. Pawn shops – If you don't feel like hassling with garage sales, eBay, Craigslist or any of that, then you can always head down to your local pawn shop and trade your stuff for cash.

99. Gold jewelry and "real" silverware – Those "Cash 4 Gold" places have been popping up all over the place for the last few years so why not take advantage of them?

If you've got gold jewelry or sterling silver silverware, you can cash in big time.

100. Musical instruments – people love buying used musical instruments because the prices on new ones are prohibitive at best. If you've got a musical instrument lying around, shine it up and clean the case. Then sell it on Craigslist for good money or head down to your local music store and get the cash even faster.

101. Resell your moving boxes – when you move, you usually spend quite a bit of money on brand new, sturdy boxes for your stuff.

There are people willing to pay you for those lightly used boxes. If you paid $200 or $300 for them, you can easily get back 50 cents on the dollar.

Here's a great resource to check out:

Boxcycle

Bonus Idea 102. Return old gifts and purchases – sometimes people get you stuff that you really don't want. Well, head on over to the store and return them.

Chapter 9
Arts & Crafts

Bonus Idea 103. Homemade Crafts – Some of us are pretty good at creating trinkets. There are plenty of market places out there that allows to sell your creativity:

Etsy (you can start yourself a little business by selling your crafts)

ArtFire (Just like Etsy. They accept both crafts and art)

Jewelrywonder (Exclusively for selling your jewelry)

Another idea is selling these crafts in tourist or busy areas in your city.

Since those areas have the highest amount of foot traffic you're bound to make some sales.

Bonus Idea 104. Craft Fairs – You can (and should) be selling your crafts online.

However, sometimes a face-to-face encounter is that much better.

You can find craft fairs in your local area by visiting:

FestivalNet.com.

105. Sell Your Art – Here's a few art marketplaces that allow you to make cash for what you probably would have been doing for fun:

DeviantArt (Sell photography, prints, and digital works)

Zazzle

Cafepress

Spreadshirt (Sell your t-shirt designs)

RedBubble These folks turn your art into posters, T-shirts, and stickers. You design it. They sell it and ship it.

Society6 (Just like RedBubble. Different name, different owners, pretty much the same audience)

Chapter 10
Ready, Set – Go!

Wow!

That was quite a list wasn't it?

Thank you for taking the time to go through it all.

Remember:
As long as you provide value, you'll ALWAYS make money.

If you haven't gotten started yet just grab 5 ideas from the list and take action on them immediately. The sooner you make the decision to take action the sooner the dollars can start rolling into your bank account.

Until next time,

Live Blessed!

Danial Barron Howe

If you feel like I've been of help to you I'd like you ask you one small a favor in return;

Please take a moment to leave a positive rating for this book with Amazon so that others will be able to benefit from it as well.

2ND EMPIRE MEDIA

See more recent titles from us

How to Write 30 Books In 30 Days

Power Profits
Cash Flow Revolution

The 10 Principals of
ENDLESS WEALTH

The 10 Principals of
IT WORKS

For our full catalog visit us at:
Wiki-Books.Com